I0158734

Printed in the United States of America.

ISBN-13: 978-1-7328082-0-1 (Paperback)

Book Cover Design by 'BJ Designs'.

Visit the author's website at www.pasttpresenttfuturee.com

Contents

Dedicated to those who are fighting to make a positive difference in the world.

Acknowledgments

"MAKE IT A HABIT TO TELL PEOPLE THANK YOU. TO EXPRESS YOUR APPRECIATION, SINCERELY AND WITHOUT THE EXPECTATION OF ANYTHING IN RETURN. TRULY APPRECIATE THOSE AROUND YOU, AND YOU'LL SOON FIND MANY OTHERS AROUND YOU. TRULY APPRECIATE LIFE, AND YOU'LL FIND THAT YOU HAVE MORE OF IT."

-RALPH MARSTON

I would like to say thank you for the people who made this book possible. Your time and dedication to this passion project of mine is greatly appreciated. I am so grateful to have you all in my life.

Thank you:

Mom and dad, for your unconditional love and support.

Robert Miller, Ashley Waterson, Linda Garcia, Sam Mamaghani, and Amanda Yoshino- My amazing editors and contributors

My talented book cover designer: BJ Designs

• • • • • • • • • • • • • • • •

Prologue

"You are dust, And to dust you
shall return."

-Genesis 3:19

Hello, Bonjour, Aloha, Hola, and So On...

What is your greatest fear?

Think about it. Long and hard.

"Wow Melina, what a deep and personal question to ask me at the beginning of the book."

I know. I know. But think about it.

Forget about the sharks and the spiders for a second. What really scares you to your very core? It is often assumed that death is the number one fear etched into the minds of human beings. But perhaps surprisingly, for most people, their most significant concern isn't dying, but rather living a life full of regrets. That's my biggest fear. That I won't live a meaningful life. That I'll miss out on an opportunity. That I'll sit on the sideline because I was too afraid to get in the game. As someone much wiser than me once said, "*I do not regret the things I've done; I regret what I did not do when I had the chance."*

What about you? Are you the individual who lives out their dreams, or the person who watches everyone else accomplish their greatest desires? Are you letting fear or doubt get in the way?

Life is well- pretty crazy that's for sure. It's full of unexpected twists and turns; ups and downs that can launch us to the highest highs or thrust us to the lowest lows. It's exhilarating at best, challenging and heartbreaking at its worst, and always complex. Every day we are faced with events and decisions that shape our experience, and all along the way we meet people whom we hope can help us make sense of the journey, or at least make the adventure worthwhile.

By writing this book, I hope to be one of those people on your journey. I have this drive to help motivate, inspire and push people to be their best selves and to keep striving for a life of meaning. I know that my readers are all at different points in their lives, but hopefully, this book and the stories and perspectives in it—both mine and others-- will have a positive impact on people at any and every stage in their life.

I don't know that this book will change your life, but writing it has certainly changed mine.

So, get in your comfy clothes—or wear your boss outfit if you'd prefer! Find a quiet corner or a noisy coffee shop, and settle in. It's time to start reading! There are some pages that I left blank for you to take notes (if that's your thing).

ALRIGHT MY DEAR READER, TAKE MY HAND LET'S GO ON AN ADVENTURE.

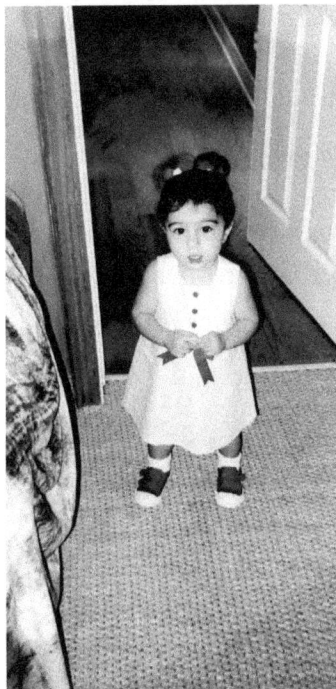

Also, look at baby me rocking this dress.

Forgive But Never Forget.

"THE STUPID NEITHER FORGIVE NOR FORGET; THE NAIVE FORGIVE AND FORGET; THE WISE FORGIVE BUT DO NOT FORGET."

-THOMAS SZASZ

A hhh forgiveness, something many of us handle poorly. Most of us struggle with forgiving those who have wronged us; but forgiveness, like love, is an essential action that should be practiced often. Now, I am not saying you should forget what people have done to you, but you also shouldn't grasp onto that anger or frustration that comes with the betrayal. At some point or another, we may feel betrayed by some of our dearest friends or most trusted family members, but it doesn't do any good to hold onto negative feelings. A few months ago, I was talking to my friend, Marilyn, on the subject of forgiveness, and she told me a very touching story about how forgiveness helped her soul find some peace. I'm going to let her take over for this…

"I never knew my father growing up. He left my mother when she was pregnant with me. Well, he didn't leave, he just umm... he didn't come back. My mom found out he was having an affair and she gave him an ultimatum: come home tonight or don't come home at all. He didn't come home that night, and when he came back the next day looking for her to take him back, she stood up for herself and told the love of her life that he had made his choice. I can't imagine the courage that must have taken.

So, he wasn't there when I came into this world, and he wasn't there for my first steps or my first words or my first day of school. He wasn't there for any firsts at all. My mom raised me by herself without ever receiving a dollar in child support from him. When I was fourteen, my mom told me they had found him. He was living in Texas in a cute house- that just looked so well put together, living this great life with a beautiful wife and two beautiful children. It was as if we never even existed. When he asked for a paternity test, I was disappointed, hurt, also.

I met him for the first time that same year. My mom and I flew out to Texas, and he met us at the airport holding a teddy bear. I was a teenager and not amused. At all. My mom and I stayed in his cute house with his beautiful wife and his beautiful children. It didn't occur to me at the time... but God, how awful that must have been for my mom. I remember feeling incredibly overwhelmed. I grew up as an only child, and now I was a big sister with a stepmom and father I didn't know at all. I tried for a few years. I made an effort to spend time with them.

They wanted to make me feel like family, but I never did. I tried to be the person they wanted me to be, but I felt like a fake because it wasn't who I was. I even flew out to visit my new family, but I just never fit in. Everything felt very unnatural to me. For instance, they were very religious. I remember they moved into a house with a pool, and on my first visit there I put on my bikini to go for a swim. I was living in Florida, I was on the swim team and was a surfer. I had a ton of bikinis and never thought anything of it. When my stepmom saw it she asked me if I had anything else to wear. When I said I didn't, she drove me to Walmart to buy a more modest swimsuit. I had never before felt ashamed in a bikini until that day. It was extremely off-putting to me at the time.

On my last visit out, I summoned the courage to ask him the one question I had always wanted an answer to:

"**H**ow could you leave us? How could you know that we were out there and move on with your life?"

His answer would dictate the next seven years of my life.

He said, "I just wasn't ready to have a kid."

No "sorry" or, "I wish I had done it differently." Just, "I wasn't ready." Any chance of a relationship with him died for me that day. I hadn't spoken to him in seven years until I got the call from my mom. I'll never forget it because six months prior, I moved out to LA to study acting and pursue my dreams. I was now in this big new city where I had no family and was starting to establish myself. I was sitting on my bed when the phone rang... I picked up, always happy to speak to my mom, and she said,

"Honey I have something to tell you."

She told me that my father, Wes, had cancer and that the doctors only gave him a few months to live.

She told me that he didn't want to tell me because he didn't want to show up in my life after seven years to say: "Well, I have cancer now- do you want to have a relation-

ship?" So he burdened her with the task. She told me she supported whatever decision I made, whether it be maintaining the lack of a relationship or wanting to make amends. She told me she loved me. During the whole time she spoke, I didn't speak a word. I was crying harder than I ever have. I could barely breathe. She just listened and told me it would be ok and that she knows. After a few minutes, I finally choked out a couple of words. **_I thought I had more time._**

T he next day I received a message on Facebook:
"I was wondering how you felt about opening up a line of communication with me? No pressure. Praying all is well with you."

I replied: "I would be really happy about it. You can call me anytime. No pressure :0)" I gave my dad my phone number.

He replied: "Okies well, I think it's great, and I'm really very happy about it as well. I have been ecstatic that you have been in Cali and am hoping that it really suits you. I'll give you a shout tomorrow night if it works for you. I can also be reached at (his phone number) whenever it might work for you. Thank you very much for....well... you know. :o)"

I never deleted the messages and still look back at them from time to time. I decided right then and there that I forgave my father because deep down inside I think I always knew we would reconcile. It was pretty ignorant because at the time I had no intention of making the first move towards repairing the relationship- I just always thought it would only happen one day. Then when I found out he was dying, I suddenly didn't care about all of the things I thought he had done wrong. I only cared about spending as much time with him as I could. I wanted to heal, but I also wanted to do it for him so that he didn't have to die with this hanging over him.

I forgave him for leaving my mom alone to raise me. I forgave him for not being there for any of my firsts. I forgave him for moving on with his life with his wife and kids. I forgave him for every little thing that I was holding against him, and I dropped everything to spend whatever time I could with him before he died. During his last few months, he was a part of many firsts. I called him "Dad" for the first time. I told him I loved him for the first time. And he told me how sorry he was for the first time. I ended up spending Christmas with him and my new family. For the first time. I got to know my brother and sister. I felt proud to be a big sister. **_So many firsts._**

I found out that my dad had cancer in October 2009 and he passed away in February of 2010. I am so grateful every day that I had those four months with him. It was like I got a lifetime of memories in the blink of an eye, and I also gained a family for life. I spoke to him on the phone the night he passed, and we were at total peace. There was a sense of unity with our relationship, and I was at peace that he was dying because we repaired the link and I had wasn't holding anything against him anymore.

N*o words had been left unsaid, and I feel blessed for the both of us every day of my life that I had the opportunity to forgive my dad before he* *passed. If I hadn't had that chance, I don't think I could have lived with it.* **It changed my life and showed me just how important forgiveness could be."**

When I first met Marilyn two years ago at a meeting for a documentary we were working on, I vividly remember being struck by what a vibrant and kind-hearted woman she was (and still is!) Let me tell you, I would've never expected hearing this story from her, because she doesn't seem like an angry or sad person. Do you know why? Because forgiving her father helped her find peace within her heart. She told me that it felt like a weight had been lifted off of her shoulders. That feeling, by the way, is incredible. Another essential thing that Marilyn pointed out is that it takes a great deal of energy to be mad at someone.

If all it takes to stop that feeling of anger and frustration is to accept the situation you are in, and allowing yourself to forgive whoever has caused you that negative feeling, then why not just do it? Don't drag it out. Holding grudges ultimately breaks you. Don't forget what they've done, but don't hold it over them forever. It's not worth it in the end. Allow your heart to have some peace.

2

Embrace the World's Greatest Gift: Diversity.

ONE BUT MANY

"ONE GOD, MANY FACES.
ONE FAMILY, MANY RACES.
ONE TRUTH, MANY PATHS.
ONE HEART, MANY COMPLEXIONS.
ONE LIGHT, MANY REFLECTIONS.
ONE WORLD, MANY IMPERFECTIONS.
ONE.
WE ARE ALL ONE,
BUT MANY."

-SUZY KASSEM, RISE UP AND SALUTE THE SUN: THE
WRITINGS OF SUZY KASSEM

HUMAN BEINGS ARE IMPERFECTLY perfect and we all have very different mindsets that are far too complex to understand. We are diverse in many ways, far more than just being diverse in ethnicity and in religious beliefs. Here are the different types of diversities that I believe we should embrace.

Number 1: Diversity in thought.

Number 2: Diversity in ethnicity.

Number 3: Diversity in religious beliefs.

BIRTHPLACE - EARTH

RACE - HUMAN

POLITICS - FREEDOM

RELIGION - LOVE

3

Do not Live to Die.

*"BELIEVE IN YOUR HEART.
BELIEVE IN YOUR HEART THAT YOU'RE MEANT TO LIVE A
LIFE FULL OF PASSION, PURPOSE, MAGIC AND MIRACLES."*

-Roy T. Bennett, '*The Light in the Heart.*'

One day you are brought into this crazy world. And one day, you are forced to grow up. You go to school and you work to get good grades so you can get into a good college. You go to a good college to get a good job that pays well. You meet someone, you get married, and you have kids. Depending on how long you live, you will watch them go through the same process. Then one day you will be no more. One day you will take your last breath and return to dust. One day it will all end.

Now imagine for just a second that you are about to take your last breath of air in this world, just imagine... how would you be reflecting on your life? Was it exciting? Was it full of twists and turns? Or did you follow the path most people go through?

Everyone knows that one day they will depart this lifetime. And I can say confidently that most people have a terrible mindset due to this piece of knowledge. They think that nothing they do matters because they will one day be gone and what they did will be meaningless. That couldn't be further from the truth. We all have a purpose. We all have a role. We all have something to contribute to this world.

For many people, they are the most powerful on the day they're born and the day they die. Why is this the case for so many people? Because many choose to sit on the sidelines of major life milestones. Because too many choose to be ordinary, and what I mean by that is that too many people follow the pack. They aren't leaders, but merely followers. I find this to be interesting because so many preach about how we need more leaders. It's also interesting because from a very young age in schools, teachers will instill this idea of being a strong leader. Yet, many don't actually follow this practice. They merely just follow what the crowd is doing.

This idea may upset some people, but it needs to be said: too many people are living ordinary lives when they have the potential and power within them to be extraordinary. I refuse to accept that our disadvantages will prevent us from succeeding in whatever goal it is we want to accomplish.

People use their obstacles and drawbacks as excuses far too often. I've been there. I can be lazy. I'm sure you can be, too. We all have our moments. But you will continue to sit on the sidelines if you aren't willing to face your fears and get into the game. You need to do this before it's too late because you only get one shot. One life. And all it takes is one moment to rise up to the challenge. It won't happen overnight, because like all things, learning to face your fears takes effort and hard work.

You are worthy. You have a power within you that will help you accomplish anything you put your mind to.

R epeat after me, *"I can and I will."*

Fun Things: Coloring Break

Take a little break to fill in this outer-space themed coloring sheet. Once you're done, resume reading the rest of the book. Give your mind some breaks when reading. Color away. See you soon.

4

Follow the 40% Rule

"When your mind is telling you you're done, you're really only 40 percent done."

-David Goggins

Navy SEAL's are some of the world's fiercest warriors, and they are known for many things, but mainly for their mental and physical toughness. The training and torture they endure show a great deal about each individual- the purpose of it all is to see who passes and who fails. A year ago, I was watching a video on *Youtube* that had featured former Navy Seal, David Goggins. He was discussing some of his most difficult challenges and was explaining the journey on how he became one of the most hardened and toughest warriors the Navy had ever seen. After watching the video, I felt this drive to push myself harder in whatever I goal I was trying to accomplish. And let me tell you, this mindset changed the game for me- especially when I went back to karate following an injury. This wasn't exactly a 'quick fix' type of thing. It completely changed my outlook and really did push me to keep going: to continue running even when I was out of breath, to keep fighting even when I was at the point of giving up. My karate teacher, who is also one of my mentors, noticed the change, and I think at the point when I told him about the mindset change, he embraced it as well. Listen, he is one of the toughest people I know… seriously- his endurance and his drive are incredible. But even the toughest people can use a mindset change and sometimes it's good to view things differently. *You are never really done when you think you are.* When times get tough during training, I will always think to myself what would David do? He would tell you to get it together and keep going.

I think everyone on the mental toughness spectrum can use a new look or a new way to view things when it comes to their mentality. People on the right side of the line (strong-minded individuals) and the people on the left side (those who need a big push) can all use a change in perspective.

When you think that you've given it all you've got, push yourself harder (but if you seriously can't breathe and think you're going to die, then just stop yourself for a minute then resume)... You have power deep within you- find it, use it, and conquer the task at hand.

5

Never Doubt the Power of the People

"The power of the people is stronger than the people in power."

-WAEL GHONIM

I was born about a month after 9/11, a tragic event that not only shook America to its very core, but also impacted the rest of the world. So many lives were ended. So many families left in its wake who would never see their loved ones again. It changed America drastically. The way we live now is greatly influenced by this heart-shattering event. 9/11 ultimately changed and created the America I and millions of others live in now. I wasn't even born when the attack happened, but it still has a huge impact on me.

We have the war on terror. And the economic crisis. And all of the millions of other problems this world is facing. My generation has only lived in a time of war and in a time of chaos. Let that sink in for a minute... What do you think that says of the generations that came before mine? In my opinion, it shows just how selfish and disgusting the human race is. However, for all of the issues we face, and for all of the evil people in the world, there are citizens around the globe fighting the good fight. And they are the reason I have even the slightest bit of hope for humanity and for the future of the human race.

The world is an oxymoron: it's imperfectly perfect. It's flawed. Incredibly flawed. We've got good humans and evil humans, and then there are the incredible humans and the terrible humans. It's a rather large scale to inspect.

And as we've seen time and time again- the world is full of evil; from terrorist attacks to mass shootings, it can often seem like the world is and will forever be screwed up. Many believe that we shouldn't do anything about it — that things won't change. I wholeheartedly disagree with those who believe this. Yes, the world is full of evil, but it's also full of good. I also need you to know that I do understand that it can seem impossible at times to make a difference and to change the world, but I have **witnessed the power of love**, and I have seen the power of the people.

I have seen first hand what we can accomplish when we work together as a united people rather than a divided group. I know that the world is incredibly messed up because of selfish beings who refuse to go face to face with reality, which is always knocking at their doors, and I know the world is filled with ill- hearted individuals who wish to inflict harm on others; however, I still believe it can and should be saved, despite everything, the world can be saved. Throughout the history of the human race, empires have risen and fallen, nations have been established, and the human race has evolved significantly. So much has happened, and so much is still to come. If we want to be around to see the incredible things future generations will accomplish, we need to work together with our young people. We need to stop criticizing others for the mistakes they have made, and learn to more forward WITH them, not against them.

I am a member of "Generation Z." Most people associate my generation with social media or the digital native age. However, I know we are far greater than that. We have the power to completely change the world for the better. More and more young people are getting involved in decision making. More and more young people are speaking up for what they believe in. And more and more young people are joining <u>the good fight</u> to save the world. I have witnessed the power of these individuals and I know that the power we hold when we are united- will push us forward in all the fights the world is facing.

Continue to fight for what you believe in, even if you're standing alone and even when all hope may seem lost. Just keep going. History can't and won't be bent by those who sit and watch the rest of the world move along while they do nothing. Keep fighting and never doubt the power within you. Don't doubt the power of the people who stand up.

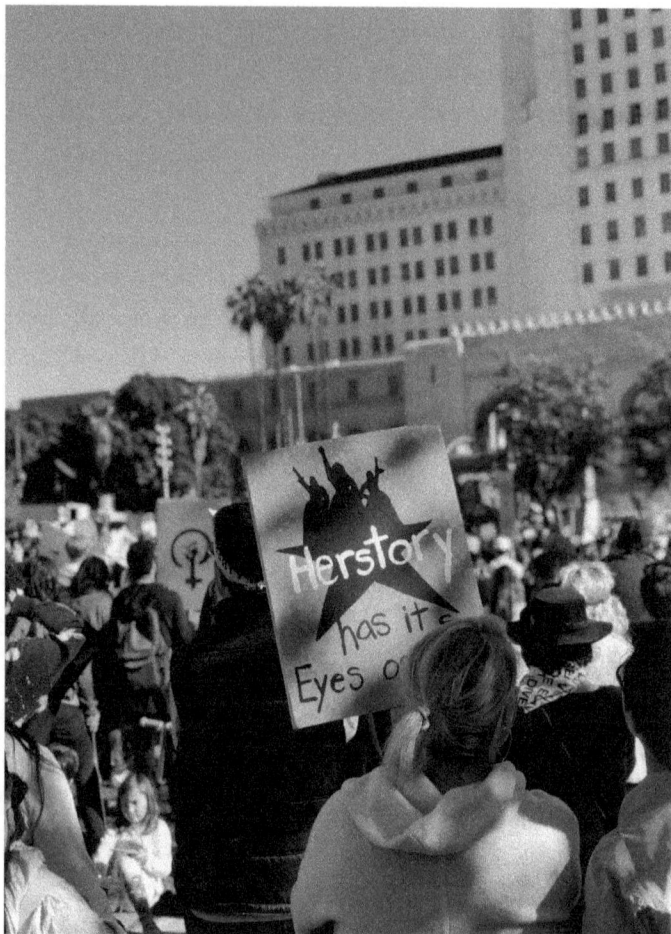

"IT FALLS TO EACH OF US TO BE THOSE ANXIOUS, JEALOUS
GUARDIANS OF OUR DEMOCRACY; TO EMBRACE THE JOYOUS
TASK WE'VE BEEN GIVEN TO CONTINUALLY TRY TO IMPROVE
THIS GREAT NATION OF OURS. BECAUSE FOR ALL OUR
OUTWARD DIFFERENCES, WE ALL SHARE THE SAME PROUD
TITLE: CITIZEN."
– Barack Obama

"Never let success get to your head
&
never let failure get to your heart."

6

Don't Waste Time Doing Things that Make You Unhappy.

"DON'T WASTE A MINUTE NOT BEING HAPPY. IF ONE WINDOW CLOSES, RUN TO THE NEXT WINDOW- OR BREAK DOWN A DOOR."

-BROOKE SHIELDS

Being born and raised in Los Angeles has taught me a lot about putting on a great act to please others who we think are better than us. And for a long time, we have this mentality that this person is amazing and really cool when in reality they are no better than you or me. People often underestimate how frequently they do certain things to please or impress other individuals. The people who have the cute designer shoes or that particular dress you saw on the runway- those things don't mean anything- it might indicate they have good taste, but it doesn't tell us anything about their character. Those material objects do not mean anything. We should all be judging others on how they treat their fellow human beings.

Another thing I've learned from living in this beautiful and sunny city is that the things that make you happy now, might not necessarily be good for you in the bigger picture. People come and go in our lives, and each of them has something to teach us- good and bad. While we have them with us, we might think it's going to last in the long run. That's not the case a lot of the time. People who I have parted ways with will always stay with me, even if they aren't physically there. The memories created will remain etched into my mind forever, but it that doesn't mean that they should necessarily be in my life again.

One thing I wish I learned earlier is that: yes, we might be having a great time with these people, but that does not mean that they are actually good for us or our happiness.

● ● ● ● ● ● ● ● ● ● ● ● ● ● ● ● ● ●

The Perfect Guy

"He was perfect. We graduated from the same college. We grew up practicing the same religion. He was a brilliant pianist, I was a singer. Everyone admired him for his talent and his kindness. Including me. We had fun together. It was perfect. When he graduated from our alma mater, a year ahead of me, he studied music at Aspen's prestigious music school over the summer, while I attended UC Berkeley. When I went to visit him, he played a song he had written for me – asking me to marry him. I said yes. We decided we would marry the following year after I graduated from college. We went ring shopping and picked out the perfect pair-shaped diamond solitaire. I spent my senior year enjoying my friendships, staying in touch with him via phone calls and frequent visits, and planning our wedding.

Things were perfect. Ok, so it wasn't so great when we went out to dinner with his parents and some friends, and they spent the entire time asking my fiancé why he wasn't still with his high school sweetheart. When we got back to his parents' house, I threw up the expensive dinner. I never throw up. I was sad that he didn't stick up for me against his mom. You see, he was her favorite – the youngest of 7 kids – because the others were too rebellious. As I met his siblings, I realized that his mom's definition of rebellious was a child who didn't let her control them. This was tempered by the fact that his father seemed to adore me.

Odd, since he was his father's least favorite of their children. His mother didn't like that either.

W*e could be so perfect. If only we got away from his parents. But the nagging thought that his mom would control our every move was never far away from my view. I came to the frightening realization that I did not want these people to be my children's grandparents when, one night while the family was out to dinner, his dad took off with one of his other grandchildren, and went down the street to a bar. The child was eighteen months old! I became less and less concerned every time we set a wedding date, his mother vetoed it, and he capitulated.*

It would be so perfect, I thought when I graduated, and we moved to Los Angeles, 300 miles away from his parents. I had overheard an argument between his mother and him about how I was following him to Los Angeles, when in fact, he was following me. He didn't correct her misconception. If only he learned to stand up against his parents. If only he was reliably upbeat. He wasn't moody, just awkward at unpredictable times. I found I was having more fun with my other friends. He was still kind, still talented, always a good person. Except for the time I had strep throat, and I was so sick, I didn't eat for 10 days. His parents came into town and whisked him away to Palm Springs.

It was a perfectly clear message when I started having nightmares about coming down the aisle to him and recoiling. But I didn't see it. When a good friend from college came into town, we met for lunch. She was staging David Bowie's show, and she brought me tickets, and a program from the show.

The image was perfect. The program had a picture of David Bowie in China Girl, laying on the beach with the actress playing a part in an intimate position. They were looking at one another, and within the intimacy of their relationship, I saw the foundation of it: Friendship. The epiphany washed over me like a tidal wave. I didn't have them with him, and I never would. I broke up with him the next day.

T*he perfect guy was now one step closer. Ten months later, I married the love of my life. Breaking up with my college sweetheart brought me closer to the one who was right for me. He's always kind. He's always funny. He would never let anyone be mean to me. His parents loved me immediately because he loved me. And I was welcomed into his family. He's my best friend, the best dad, the best husband I could ever ask for. I am so grateful that I saw clearly – in time – that my fiancé and I weren't right for one another. I still care about him. We are still friendly. I still want him to be happy. I wish only the best for him. Ten years later, he married a beautiful girl, with whom he has two children. They are happy, and that makes me happy.*

T*URNS OUT HE WAS PERFECT ... FOR SOMEONE ELSE.*"

-Lynn Holmgren

• • • • • • • • • • • • • • • •

Something I learned from this story is that we need to pay attention to the signs life is giving us. If you are unhappy with a particular situation you are in- take a step back, analyze the issues, and make an assessment on how to proceed. Not only that, it is also important to check in with yourself, your mental health is important and your happiness should be a priority in your life.

7

Stand for Something, or You'll Fall for Nothing.

"*IF YOU STAND FOR SOMETHING YOU WILL HAVE PEOPLE*
FOR YOU AND PEOPLE AGAINST YOU.
BUT IF YOU STAND FOR NOTHING YOU WILL HAVE
NOBODY FOR YOU,
AND NOBODY AGAINST YOU."
-MAURICE SAATCHI

There's always something happening in the world, whether it be good or bad- and people aren't always paying close attention to the negative aspect. Human beings often times choose not to do anything about issues that can eventually cause problems for them because some people feel that it isn't their problem when in reality it is. When we are silent on issues that matter we are no better than those who are causing the problem.

I became a very vocal activist when I was in seventh grade. Learning to speak up for what was right completely transformed me as a person, and I am so happy that I found that courage within me to do so. I wrote my first letter to a political leader in seventh grade as well. Little did I know that months later I would receive a heart-warming message back from President Barack Obama- one of my biggest inspirations in the fight for a better future and a better America. So I continued... In 2014 I created a website with the goal of empowering women, and at the time I wrote mainly about fashion and beauty. Once I started developing my "warrior voice" as I call it, I then changed it to a multi purpose website dedicated to multiple topics such as: fashion, beauty, lifestyle, empowerment, and politics.

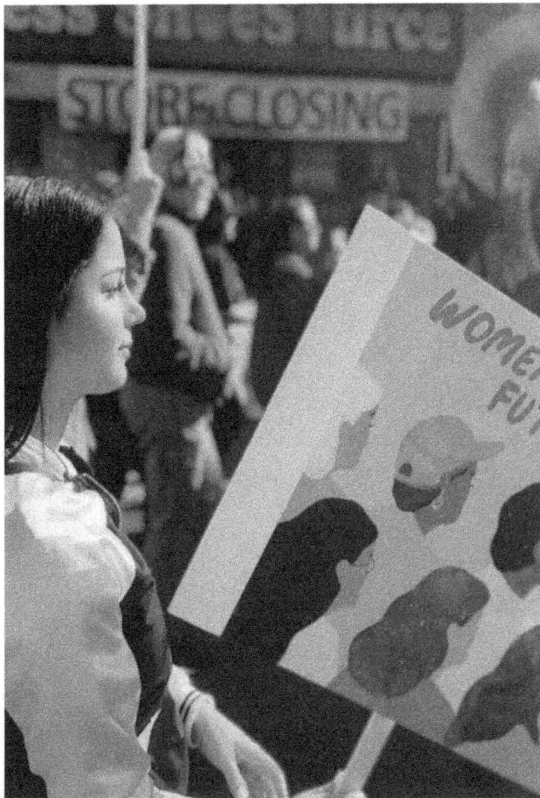

Women's March 2018

I started writing... a lot. Discussing crucial world issues and raising awareness was something that I took very seriously. Multiple pieces I've written have been published in magazines, and the responses to those articles kept pushing me even further. It felt great to finally have a voice. The more and more issues I wanted to raise awareness about meant more letters being written to politicians. Receiving letters back always reaffirmed my belief in speaking up for what I believed in. After several months, I received multiple messages from Senator Kamala Harris and Senator Dianne Feinstein, and even a letter from Representative Ted Lieu. One letter in particular that I will always treasure is a letter from First Lady Michelle Obama... Now that was something else. The common theme in all of their messages had to do with continuing to fight for what I believed in. And I realized that my purpose as a human being and as a woman was to fight for those who can't. To speak up for what is right. To make a difference in the world.

I have attended both Women's Marches in Los Angeles and being there, marching for what I believed in, standing up with my fellow women (and men) was one of the most liberating feelings I've ever experienced.

What I stand for says a tremendous amount about me as a person. What I stand up for, will ultimately go down with my legacy when I am gone. The same thing applies to you as well. Find something that you adamantly believe in and want to defend with every fiber of your being. People will not always agree with what you think in (that's just how life goes), but what matters is that you stand up for something great.

Fun Things: Highlighter Time

THE FIRST 3 WORDS YOU SEE ARE
WHAT YOU WANT IN LIFE:

```
X  C  U  A  L  O  V  E  Y  K  B  W  S  N  G
D  U  A  W  K  C  B  E  A  U  T  Y  R  J  V
Y  O  U  T  H  F  S  M  G  N  E  Z  L  P  R
M  H  J  R  E  Y  W  D  K  Z  L  U  S  T  J
F  S  U  C  C  E  S  S  D  H  E  A  L  T  H
E  N  M  Q  X  P  T  I  M  E  L  M  S  A  Q
V  E  X  P  E  R  I  E  N  C  E  G  H  B  W
G  H  U  M  O  U  R  L  O  Y  M  O  N  E  Y
S  Y  Z  P  O  P  U  L  A  R  I  T  Y  N  A
A  M  K  C  F  U  N  B  X  H  U  Z  Y  I  X
C  W  I  H  Y  S  H  A  P  P  I  N  E  S  S
H  O  N  E  S  T  Y  C  F  R  I  E  N  D  S
K  P  Y  J  A  E  T  W  P  O  W  E  R  Q  C
B  T  Y  A  C  F  R  E  E  D  O  M  J  M  O
R  I  W  I  N  T  E  L  L  I  G  E  N  C  E
```

8

Look for Beautiful Minds,
Not Faces.

"IN THE END WE WON'T REMEMBER THE MOST BEAUTIFUL FACE AND BODY. WE'LL REMEMBER THE MOST BEAUTIFUL HEART AND SOUL."

-UNKNOWN

A s I'm writing this chapter, I am currently watching an episode of a show called *"Black Mirror"* on *Netflix*, specifically the episode starring the beautiful and talented Bryce Dallas Howard. The episode was called '*Nosedive*,' and the two major themes that I noticed are more important than some may realize: don't be somebody you aren't just to please society, and look for people who whose characters are beautiful, not (just) their faces.

In this episode, Bryce Dallas Howard plays Lacie, a kind-hearted woman with the distasteful obsession with becoming popular— specifically having a 4.5 star rating on social media. It was actually an unfortunate/sad episode, to say the least; it hit me hard. One of the themes discussed was people's infatuation with social media and how we judge others based on their likes and number of followers. The other thing was how we all act fake with each other, or "ass kissing" as it is commonly referred to here in Los Angeles, a beautiful city filled with "Hollywood people"…

Now, when I say the term "Hollywood people," I'm not talking about the actors or directors and everyone who's a part of this industry. I'm talking about the people who say in their high-pitched voice while sipping an espresso,

"Oh My God! It has been forever since I've seen you! Let's get together for lunch, babe."

I've heard this phrase time and time again from Hollywood friends, and I always smile politely and say sure! But inside the complex world, which is my mind, I'm thinking, please, kindly f—off. But I would never say that out loud, we have to stay classy after all (*cue smirk on my face*).

What I'm trying to say is, don't let the number of likes and followers, or the Hollywood friend with a pretty face, dictate how you live your life. It's not worth it. We spend too much time obsessed with how we look in the eyes of others, and we never stop to acknowledge what it's doing to our mental health. Just stop! Spend time with people you actually and genuinely like for who they are, not only because they are popular. Spend time with those who are smart, kind, and have a beautiful heart, not just a beautiful face.

This episode of *Black Mirror* really opened my eyes to how unaware people are about things that really matter. Never compromise your happiness just to satisfy some social standard. My mom always said terrible friends will bring you down. By that she meant, choose your friends wisely because they reflect the type of person you are.

For example, if you are friends with someone who is shallow and disrespectful, then that calls into question the type of person you are for choosing them as a friend... The bottom line is: Look for individuals with beautiful minds and souls, not (only) beautiful faces.

WARNING:

Reflections in this mirror may be distorted by socially constructed ideas of 'beauty'

9

No Overtime in Life

"*Don't think twice. We have been given a gift that we call life. So don't blow it. You're not defined by your past instead you were born anew in each moment. So own it now. Sometimes you've got to leap and grow your wings on the way down. You better get the shot off before the clock runs out because <u>there ain't no overtime in life</u>, no do-over. And I know that it sounds like I'm preaching or speaking with force, but if you don't use your gift, then you sell not only yourself but the whole world...short.*

So what invention do you have buried in your mind? What idea?

What cure? What skill do you have inside to bring out to this universe?

UNI MEANING ONE, VERSE MEANING SONG. YOU HAVE A PART TO PLAY IN THIS SONG.

SO GRAB THAT MICROPHONE AND BE BRAVE. SING YOUR HEART OUT ON LIFE'S STAGE. YOU CANNOT GO BACK AND MAKE A BRAND NEW BEGINNING. BUT YOU CAN START NOW AND MAKE A BRAND NEW ENDING."

-Prince EA

People try so many different things to live a longer life, and to increase their time on earth. It is as if the number of years they have is so significant. You see, what people fail to realize is that it should never be about how many years you live. It's not about living to a hundred. Life is not about the number of years, but rather the quality of your years. Before you die, make sure you've lived.

My friend Allyson, a brave and vibrant woman who survived colon cancer, often discusses this topic with me. She also happens to write about her fight with cancer on my website, where she is a lifestyle and empowerment writer. Allyson was telling me the story about when she first found out she had cancer and how her outlook and perspective on life were drastically altered.

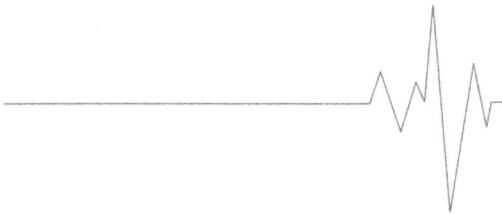

Death The Ultimate Motivator

"The best way to begin living a healthy, joyful, purpose-driven life is to start dying—I mean like really dying—not the "Well, we are dying a little bit every day" dying but the "OMG! I AM DYING." **I am dying** *. . .*

Dying will make you want to live more than ever before. Dying will make sure your priorities are straight, your goals redefined, your grudges forgiven, and your dreams fueled with a force more powerful than you've ever imagined.

When you are dying and time is running out, your mind is frantic, as if your house is on fire and you have 15 minutes to get what you want and leave the rest behind. At that point, you don't think about which pair of Christian

Louboutin's or Chanel handbag to save, you think about the most valuable things. I'm not talking about value as in currency. I'm talking about heart value: your children, your pets, the ring your mother passed down to you from her mother, the gold cross that your father gave to you on the day that you were confirmed, the handprint collage your children made for you in kindergarten on old construction paper. These things are of no value to anyone except you because these are the things that made you who you are.

I was 42 when I was diagnosed with stage-three colon cancer. My daughter, Sophia Lovina, was six. My son, Connor Elvis, was four. And I... I was dying. It was a Friday afternoon in February, and my doctor said she needed to see me right away. "But it's Friday, and it's rush hour... in Los Angeles!" Oh, I thought to myself.

"I... have... cancer." Boy, did I have cancer: one stage away from death.

My blood was rushing as I'd never felt before, and my heart was beating double-time. I could feel every muscle, hear every sound, and see more clearly than ever. ***I was ALIVE.*** *The moment I found out I was dying was the moment I felt the most alive. Ironic, isn't it?*

Nearly in a catatonic state, I watched, looking down on myself from above as if I was starring in a slow-mo movie, not a role I'd ever want to play by the way. I was moved briskly from one place to another. Blood tests and other tests. Who knows? It was all a blur. There were mounds of paperwork, and my signature was required everywhere. What did I sign? I didn't know. I didn't care.

"I DON'T CARE. I'm dying."

That was the most extended weekend of my life. It was a pre-Valentines' Day weekend, and love was in the air. My love, my loves were in my air, in my breath, in my eyes, mouth, ears, blood, veins, mind, heart, spirit, and every fiber in my body. Terror.

Wait a minute – am I going to be that mom making videos for her daughter about becoming a woman, getting a good education, marrying a man of substance, respecting herself, and giving generously? Sharing my wishes for her through a laptop, advising her to stand up always for what she believes in, no matter what. Listen to your inside voice. You were named after Sophia Loren because she is classy, sophisticated, and full of grace. Embrace those qualities for they will serve you well. Sophia means "wisdom," and you are naturally, by fate, an academic. Use your intellect to make a difference for those who can't. Laugh. Love your children as I've loved you. You are an incredible child.

Then to my son: Be honorable and courageous. Be chivalrous, and make sure that you open the door for your girlfriend. Choose a wife who will love you unconditionally. Your children are treasures, the most precious of all gifts, so take good care of them and make the time to show up. Treat all people equally, and be kind and generous. Already, you show signs of becoming a gifted athlete. Be the quarterback that others look up to, not fear. Be the example, not the cliché. Protect the weak, the geeks, and the underdogs. Don't swear. Do not be hard on yourself. Laugh. Love your children as I've loved you. You are a fantastic child.

And, to both of you, take care of one another and always say your prayers. There will be times when you will need God, and He will be there for you.

I will forever be with you. Always. I love you forever. Mommy.

N *O! "Oh my God. Please, God—Please, please, please, God—please, please, please, PLEASE DO NOT TAKE ME AWAY... FROM THEM. PLEASE." All I cared about was not leaving Sophia and Connor. How is this possible? I just gave birth to them not too long ago. I don't want to leave them. I won't. I'm not. I'm not leaving them. NO. Even now, as I write this, my eyes fill up, and my heart hurts. It is PAIN worse than any other pain. They are my reasons. They will always be my reasons. They are my reasons for being here.*

The moment I realized I was dying was the moment I decided to LIVE.

At that point, my life path was in entertainment. I grew up in Vancouver, beautiful British Columbia, and had already achieved tremendous success as a dancer, model, and actress in Canada. My dream was to go to a school like in the TV series, [FAME]. Beyond thrilled, I was awarded a scholarship to the American Academy of Dramatic Arts, so I packed my bags and left my beloved hometown to embrace my dream and live it to the fullest. After that, I wrote and acted in many projects. That's when the Grim Reaper came knocking on my door. All bets and TV shows were off.

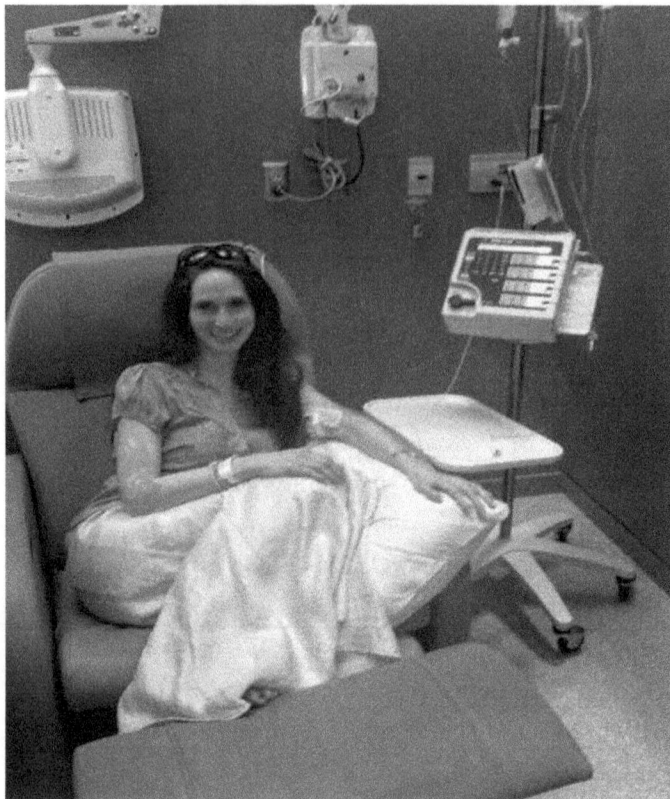

I entered the world of cancer, and there are really no words to describe the emotional, mental, and physical pain one must go through to LIVE, but during this "journey," as it is often referred to, I changed. There was a shift, and it moved me like a 9.9 earthquake. What is this all about? What is my purpose? What legacy will I leave behind when I have to make my final curtain call? My profound questions were now crystal clear.

My decision was definite and made the day I was diag-

nosed. As I lay on my bed, staring at the ceiling and having that earnest talk with the big guy, I decided that I was going to give back once I conquered this beast, and I was going to give back BIG. It was not a bargaining tool, "If you let me live, God, I'll do this," and it was not fear to talk either; it was just a simple shift. At that moment, I felt such peace and contentment. I felt that my purpose was finally defined, and I was ready to fulfill my new declaration.

Post-surgery—the first surgery, that is—my surgeon, Dr. Sack, sat beside me while I held him captive, outlining all the things I was going to do once I was "finished." I told him about how I was going to mentor people through cancer and publish interviews with doctors, survivors, health and wellness professionals, and anyone who can be a supportive resource when it comes to information, inspiration, and insight into the world of cancer.

And I did. I am now a certified cancer coach, life coach, health and wellness coach, and a professional inspirational speaker. I am also the founder of Colon Cancer Women, a 501c3 non-profit that I'm building with the support of the most decent, honorable, and incredible people.

Looking back, I feel that the toolset I mastered during my years of studying, creating, producing, and performing was crafted for this moment. I feel so grateful to be able to give back to the world of cancer treatment, to empower others to get through no matter how difficult, and to make a valuable difference in people's lives.

Having cancer is what I call a backward blessing, and death was the ultimate motivator.

Am I healthy, joyful, and purpose-driven in life? YES!

The definition of grateful: appreciative of benefits received. My benefits are endless, from a constant stream of warm water and a bathtub to a roof over my head and food to eat. By nature, I am a grateful person, but when you are dying gratitude is magnified because your world is small and your wants simple: to able to get out of bed, swallow your medication, spend quality time with your children, and have just one more day. Every day is only one more day to be alive.

N*ow, here I am on the other side, and my sense of gratitude has not diminished. Daily devotion: "Thank you God for this beautiful day, for health, my children's health and for your guidance in our lives. Please use me to serve others through your light and love deeply. Thank you for LIFE."*

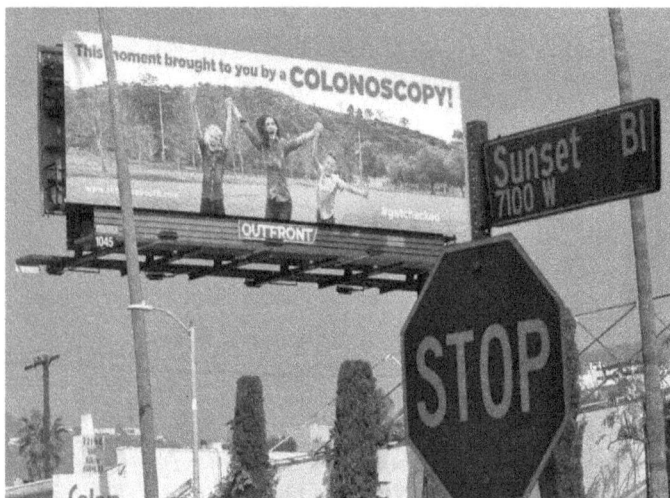

The magic we experience every day goes unnoticed for most people: our heart that never misses a beat, and how our blood flows through our body like a mysterious melody, how we fall asleep and then wake up automatically—how we blink and smile and cry and laugh and breathe without ever even thinking about it. Yes, it's true, it is the little things in life and the big things too. When perfectly combined, we are complete.

The reason why people who come back from near-

*death experiences feel so very lucky is that they now know the truth. Death is the darkness that pushes you into the light of LIFE. What I have learned about my mortality is that I am not invincible or in control... of anything. **Every single day is the most incredible day of my life, and I live it like I'm dying.***"

. . . .

Very few people have a second chance to change the way they live their lives. Don't wait until death is knocking on the door to turn things around. You have one shot and one chance only. Don't sit on the sidelines when you can get in the game.

You will fail, and honestly, you will fail often in life. There will be days where you'll want to give up. Days that will make you examine and question everything. Keep going. Accomplish your dreams. Listen to the signs that the universe is showing you. The cosmos are a unique gift we've been provided.

Listen to your soul and listen to your mind. The only thing that will matter at the end of the day is that you tried and that you got off the ground and persisted. You have one chance, and one chance only. **Don't remain on the sidelines when you can get in the game.** And once you're in the game, persevere and work vigorously. There's only one round, and **no overtime will be granted**. You have one shot to go out there and conquer your fears and to accomplish your dreams. Don't sell yourself or the world short. You have multiple gifts within you that are waiting to be unlocked. There is only so much time... so little time. People think they have all the time in the world to do things, but really- they don't. The truth is we really don't have much time. Don't miss your shot.

10

Change One Soul's Life
Everyday

*" **THAT GREAT PARAGON OF ANALYTICAL RIGOR, ASK.COM,
SAYS THAT THE AVERAGE AMERICAN WILL MEET 10,000
PEOPLE IN THEIR LIFETIME. THAT'S A LOT OF FOLKS. BUT,
IF EVERY ONE OF YOU CHANGED THE LIVES OF JUST 10
PEOPLE — AND EACH ONE OF THOSE FOLKS CHANGED THE
LIVES OF ANOTHER 10 PEOPLE — JUST 10 — THEN IN
FIVE GENERATIONS — 125 YEARS — THE CLASS OF 2014
WILL HAVE CHANGED THE LIVES OF 800 MILLION PEOPLE.
800 MILLION PEOPLE — THINK OF IT — OVER TWICE THE
POPULATION OF THE UNITED STATES. GO ONE MORE
GENERATION AND YOU CAN CHANGE THE ENTIRE
POPULATION OF THE WORLD — EIGHT BILLION PEOPLE. "***

- EXCERPT FROM ADMIRAL WILLIAM MCRAVEN'S
COMMENCEMENT 2014 SPEECH.

WE ALL HAVE the power to change the world, and some-times the first step to improving the world for the better starts by changing at least one person's life every day.

People often underestimate and undervalue the power of kindness or the uncomplicated act of asking someone how their day is going, or even just smiling at a stranger. It is astonishing how such a simple action can make some-one's day better. If all of us were actually to believe in the power of love and compassion, we would be one step closer to making a positive impact in the world. Here's the key to changing a person's life, every single day: carry out an act of kindness. The best part? It won't cost you a thing. It's free. And it will make your heart feel a whole lot fuller.

Whether it be a stranger or someone in your life, people need to be reminded that there is someone out there who loves and cares about them. I make it a priority to text people at the beginning and end of the week to check in and see how they are doing and also to tell them that I hope they have a great day. I may not always get to do it, but I really do try to make sure that I do that in the morning. What matters is that I am checking in on them, which is my way of showing them that: '*Yes, I do care about your well being,*' and it also reminds them that there is someone out there who cares. Who honestly cares. It's the little things that can make all the difference. **If you want to make a difference in the world, carry out a kind act every day.** It will make you feel like a better human being, and it can change someone else's life.

While we are on the subject of improving people's lives I would also like to add this: never let people feel abandoned or lonely. Please please please listen to me and take this seriously… Loneliness is such a dreadful thing. And sometimes for many, the case is that they have a lot of people around them, but no one who is genuinely there for them. No one who is indeed present. Check in on people. Remind them that they are loved. It should be a continuous act: once won't be enough- it has to be done regularly. And when they see you reaching out to them, they may also continue that act and carry it on to others.

You should make it your mission to check in on loved ones- even the ones who seem really tough, because I know that even they need someone to check in on them. Be that person. Carry out a kind act everyday. It is the first and easiest step to changing the world for the better.

• • • • • • • • • • • • • • • •

"Place your hands
into soil to feel
grounded. Wade in
water to feel
emotionally
healed. Fill your
lungs with fresh
air to feel
mentally clear.
Raise your face to
the heat of the sun
and connect with
that fire to feel
your own immense
power."

— Victoria Erickson,
    Rebelle Society

11

Be Kind to People, Even if They Don't Deserve it.

"It's not our job to play judge and jury, to determine who is worthy of our kindness and who is not. We just need to be kind, unconditionally and without ulterior motive, even - or rather, especially - when we'd prefer not to be."

- Josh Radnor

YEAH YEAH... I know. It's easier to be a smart-ass when someone is being rude to us. I get it. But at the end of the day, if we choose the path of hatred and nasty remarks, we are no better than our enemies and we will be no better than those who have wronged us. Always pause and ask yourself.... *Is this really worth it?* Ask yourself that question the next time someone is rude to you. I am not saying that you shouldn't speak up for yourself or others, but there are better ways to deal with annoying humans.

Kindness is always the best route to travel through. And trust me, I know it can be difficult to hold your tongue when someone says something rude or disrespectful to you. I've been there... But, like my grandfather taught me from a very young age, we should always treat others with the kindness we wish to receive back. We won't exactly receive that kindness back if we are rude, unkind, or disrespectful.

"choose you, choose love, and choose the people who stand for something and make a difference... because you were born to do so. you are here to set things on fire and set them free."

— *r. m. drake*

Fun Things: Coloring Part 2

12

Learn from Your Past and Move Forward.

"THE PAST CAN HURT. BUT THE WAY I SEE IT, YOU CAN EITHER RUN FROM IT OR LEARN FROM IT."

- Rafiki, *The Lion King*

This lesson ties back to the whole concept of forgiveness; however, instead of forgiving others, you are learning to forgive yourself for any mistakes YOU have made. As human beings, we make mistakes often, very often. But I think it's an essential part about actually being a part of humanity- the most flawed species to ever walk the earth. The mistakes made in the past should stay right there, in the past. What you should take forward with you are the lessons learned from those little screw ups. Said something you shouldn't have to a friend? Well, it was, and you can't take it back. Did you ever apologize? Yes? Then that's a great start. No? Well... you may need to address that. What's the lesson learned here? Well, there are two lessons I can learn from the example: think before you speak, and remember to be kind. You may find more lessons from this example, and that's great.

And let's quickly shift gears for a second- remember to always THINK before you open your mouth. Ask yourself if what you're about to say may hurt the other person's feelings. If it's something you wouldn't want you parents to hear, then you probably shouldn't say it. A very straight-forward concept.

Moving back to the whole topic on the past. Everything you've done in your past, is your past. You can't change it, but you can learn from it. You are going to make mistakes and those mistakes will ultimately help you in the long run. Everything you've done in the past and everything you're doing now, will ultimately shape you into who you're going to be.

The past has passed, learn to let it go.

"The past doesn't define us. It just gives US a starting point for who we're going to be."

13

Respect is a Core Value that Should be Taught and Practiced Everyday.

"I SPEAK TO EVERYONE IN THE SAME WAY, WHETHER HE IS THE GARBAGE MAN OR THE PRESIDENT OF THE UNIVERSITY."

—ALBERT EINSTEIN

When we treat ourselves and others with respect, people will respect you (well.... most of the time). It always bothers me when people my age are disrespectful to teachers, elders, etc... overall it bothers me when anyone is disrespectful to another individual, but it really aggravates me when children and teens think they're better than adults, and think they can just disrespect them. Take a seat sweetie. You are not there yet.

I will never understand human beings desire to treat others like garbage. We are all members of the human race. We allow things like gender or social class determine how we view/judge people.

"WE ARE SUN AND MOON, DEAR FRIEND; WE ARE SEA AND LAND. IT IS NOT OUR PURPOSE TO BECOME EACH OTHER; IT IS TO RECOGNIZE EACH OTHER, TO LEARN TO SEE THE OTHER AND HONOR HIM FOR WHAT HE IS: EACH THE OTHER'S OPPOSITE AND COMPLEMENT."
— HERMANN HESSE, NARCISSUS AND GOLDMUND

Every time I read this quote, I remember something my mom said to me when I was younger, "we all came from the same place, and we are all going to the same place." Out of all of the things my mom has taught me this is high up on the list titled 'Wise Things Mom Says.' Because she's right. It's a hard concept for so many people to grasp that we should all treat each other as equals and with respect rather than act like we are superior beings. News-flash humans, we kinda suck sometimes. Well... most of the time.

My martial arts instructor, who also happens to be my mentor and one of my closest friends discusses the impor-tance of respecting everyone and everything often in class. He and I will frequently discuss this topic during our morning runs. I was raised on the foundation that respect must earned, but it should also be practiced regardless of who we are speaking to. Whether it's the principal of the school or the janitor cleaning the halls. Respect must be given to everyone. It is in the handbook of being a decent human being. My martial arts instructor (who I mentioned earlier), and friend for the last decade, Matt Emery explains respect so eloquently:

"One of the most important martial artists in the world once told me, "martial arts are built on the foundation of respect, loyalty, honesty, and integrity." These are beautiful words of wisdom from a truly incredible individual. I learned a lot from this partic-ular teacher over the years - boxing, kickboxing, grap-pling, weapons techniques, self-defense tactics and more. Though all of these drills and exercises are important and valuable, it's the life lessons that I learned from this man that will stay with me forever. This particular teacher *inspired me to always do my best in everything that I do. He was the type of instructor who helped you to be a better martial artist, and more importantly, he was the type of instructor who helped you to be a better human. It was his deep level of kindness and respect for others (along with a deep understanding of the importance of friendship and a one-of-a-kind welcoming spirit) that drew people into his Ohana, or family. I have always been a very respectful individual, however, whenever I had the opportunity and honor of working with this teacher, I felt the desire to expand my level of respect even further. This dedication eventually led me to being recognized and presented the award of "Most Respectful" among his students, at our annual Instructor's Conference. A true honor.*

As a martial arts instructor, I have the privilege to act as a guide for my students as they travel on the martial arts path. The martial arts journey has many twists and turns, and all along the way, there are great lessons to be learned. I have been blessed with an ability to communicate and understand children. My job is to inspire them to

be the very best that they can be, in all areas of life, in and out of the Martial Arts Academy. This is a responsibility that I take very seriously.

The students and I learn from each other. We continually have meaningful discussions on a variety of topics such as life skills, health and safety tips, kindness and compassion, being courageous, practicing perseverance and of course, respect. As one of the foundations of the martial arts, the theme of respect and honor comes up on a daily basis - respect for your family, respect for others, respect for yourself, respect for nature... respect for all.

Parents, from time to time, will ask me to discuss particular topics that their child may need a little extra help with. I am, of course, happy to help in any way that I can. One of the topics that is requested regularly is that of respect. It would appear that we are living in a time where it is challenging to raise kids. Everyone is over-scheduled, the lure of electronic screens is ever present, and it seems that all too often, disrespectful language, attitudes, and behavior is tolerated or even celebrated (in movies, music,

social media, etc.). This, in turn, may cause a child to act disrespectfully toward his or her family, friends or teachers. This is unfortunate and unacceptable.

As parents, we must work hard and go above and beyond to instill moral values and virtues in our children. This is of utmost importance. We must also learn to become excellent listeners and set an example of good behavior. Everyone can improve in this area.

We must teach our children, no matter what their age, the value of respect. As a martial artist, I will always go back to the basics. In this case, speaking in a kind manner, with appropriate words, in a pleasant tone of voice is an excellent place to start, if we want to set a good example for our children. Practicing good manners and remembering to say things such as, "please," "thank you very much," "you're welcome," "excuse me," and "I'm sorry," will go a long way in helping kids (and parents) develop a respectful attitude while enhancing their capacity for kindness, compassion, and empathy. This simple and pure life skill, when practiced, will have benefits that are far reaching.

When I reflect and think about the martial arts instructor mentioned above, I am reminded of just how grateful I am to have known him. I am also reminded of how much I miss him, as he passed suddenly last year. His name is Grandmaster Richard Bustillo - one of Bruce Lee's top students and a teacher, mentor, and friend to countless top martial artists around the world. We honor his legacy by passing the lessons that he taught us, on to the next generation - a gesture of love and respect. The teachings of "respect, loyalty, honesty, and integrity," must be taught. If *we can teach our kids, while setting a good example ourselves, we can all do our part in helping to make the world a better place."*

"I bow in respect..."

Matt Emery with Grandmaster Richard Bustillo

14

Never go to Bed Angry at
Someone.

"NEVER GO TO BED ANGRY, STAY UP AND FIGHT."
-William Congreve

Y ou never know what life is going to throw at you and you don't ever want your last conversation with someone to be an argument over something stupid. Not only that, but going to bed with a negative attitude and mindset will only give you and your body unnecessary stress and anger.

I don't have any story that goes along with this lesson. It is just a rule that should be followed. If the issue isn't being resolved, be the bigger person and be the one who instigates the conversation about forgiveness. If the matter that you and another person are trying to solve is much more than a silly fight, make a deal with each other that you will discuss the issue the next day and that you will remain kind until then. There's always room for negotiations, learn to compromise. But under no circumstances should you go to bed angry at a person.

15

You Must be at Your Very Best, Even in Your Darkest Moments.

"IF YOU WANT TO CHANGE THE WORLD, YOU MUST BE YOUR VERY BEST IN THE DARKEST MOMENT.
-AT THE DARKEST MOMENT OF THE MISSION IS THE TIME WHEN YOU MUST BE CALM, COMPOSED—WHEN ALL YOUR TACTICAL SKILLS, YOUR PHYSICAL POWER AND ALL YOUR INNER STRENGTH MUST BE BROUGHT TO BEAR."

-ADMIRAL WILLIAM MCRAVEN
(UNITED STATES NAVY, RETIRED).

I t's easy to freak out and to panic during your darkest moments when you are experiencing fear.

I totally understand that it is a normal human reaction, but I just find it to be a bit ridiculous when people make the situation they are in a hundred times worse than it actually is. You have to master the act of staying calm and collected during extreme conditions. First and foremost, learn breathing techniques. Your heart rate tends to spike, and your breathing becomes irregular when you are scared so if you can learn to control your breathing pattern, and are familiar with the practice of "managing" your heart rate, you are set. Second, analyze the situation you are in. What's going on exactly? What can you do to defuse the problem?

I have anxiety, so I know it can be hard for people who also have it to control themselves enough to calm themselves down. However, this is something that will take practice and won't change overnight. You are going to have to work at it. But this is something that should be worked on.

You have to be strong, and somewhere within you, that strength is there.

Fun Things: Complex Coloring

16

Create a Legacy Worth Remembering.

"LEGACY. WHAT IS A LEGACY? IT'S PLANTING SEEDS IN A GARDEN YOU NEVER GET TO SEE."

-HAMILTON MUSICAL

W riting this final chapter and discussing this valuable lesson is really one of the main reasons I wrote this book in the first place. To help you and others learn. Learn to be better people. Better learners. Better warriors. Better human beings. Just like the world, humans are imperfectly perfect. You never know what's going on inside their heads, but sure enough, it's bound to be a complex world in there. We are all very different in a variety of ways, but one thing that unites us is our desire to leave our mark on the planet, *to not be forgotten.* One of my favorite topics to discuss with people is about legacies and passions, and what we want to accomplish in life.

. . . .

So, what exactly is a legacy? The first thing everyone should know is: we don't get to see our legacies, but we create them. It's not really about physical stuff you leave behind, like a house or jewelry for your kids- it's about the feeling you leave INSIDE of people's hearts. A legacy is about how you impact people.

Here is a motto to embrace: live the way you want to be remembered. In other words, the golden rule, treat others the way you want to be treated. Your mark on the world should be impactful. Your impact can be something extraordinary, or it can be for something simple that made people happier; in reality, all that matters it that you did. Just another something to think about.

"EVERYONE MUST LEAVE SOMETHING BEHIND WHEN HE DIES . . . SOMETHING YOUR HAND TOUCHED SOME WAY, SO YOUR SOUL HAS SOMEWHERE TO GO WHEN YOU DIE . . . IT DOESN'T MATTER WHAT YOU DO, SO LONG AS YOU CHANGE SOMETHING FROM THE WAY IT WAS BEFORE YOU TOUCHED IT INTO SOMETHING THAT'S LIKE YOU AFTER YOU TAKE YOUR HANDS AWAY."

-Ray Bradbury, Fahrenheit 451

What we leave behind means everything about who we were. You must leave something good behind that isn't physical. Something that will stay etched into people's minds and souls. The things we leave within people are meant to be remembered forever, and the idea is that they will pass along your teachings and your memories to others.

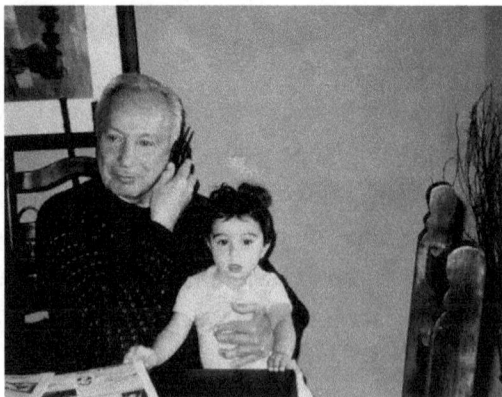

"Stories have to be told or they die, and when they die, we can't remember who we are or why we're here."

- SUE MONK KIDD

If You Want to Change
the World

"Start each day with a task completed. Find someone to help you through life. Respect everyone.

Know that life is not fair and that you will fail often. But if take you take some risks, step up when the times are toughest, face down the bullies, lift up the downtrodden and never, ever give up — if you do these things, then the next generation

and the generations that follow will live in a world far better than the one we have today. And what started here will indeed have changed the world — for the better."

-Admiral William McRaven
(United States Navy, Retired).

Fun Things: Coloring Break Pt. 3

17

Final Words and Goodbyes

Farewell, Goodbye, Aloha, Adios….

Y ou have now come to the end of this book, and it's time to say for us to say goodbye. Writing this book has given me a piece of freedom. The freedom that I have always needed. It has helped me share lessons that I hope more people will follow. In a way, I feel liberated, and it's a great feeling.

I genuinely hope that these lessons will help improve your life in some way and that you've learned something from what I had to say, and I really mean that from the bottom of my heart. I have always wanted to be someone people can look up to and for as long as I could remember, I have wanted to create a legacy that people will look back on. I think we all should really... because we really don't know when we are going to leave this Earth, but if you were told that you only had one day left to live, would you be satisfied with the legacy you are leaving behind? Would people remember you as someone who spoke up for what was right? As someone who lived life to the fullest?

Is there going to be someone who will continue your legacy? Who will tell your story? And ultimately, whoever does tell your story: will that be a story of how you did good and how you lived a life led by love and compassion? Ask yourself these questions...

So my dear reader, if today was your last day on Earth would you be satisfied with the life you have lived? If the answer is no, then I suggest you change that situation and start living. Start living a life that makes you happy. An experience that will be worth remembering, even when you are gone.

Today is life, and as far as we know, it's the only life we are sure of. It is up to you to decide how you want to live this life. The time we have on this earth is limited, and it would be a shame if you didn't live a life full of purpose and meaning, and it would be an even greater shame if you ended up realizing that when it's too late. It would really be the biggest mistake you will ever make.

Check off some of the boxes on your bucket list. Surround yourself with good people with good souls and beautifully complex minds. Take some risks and have fun (but seriously never do drugs, that's a no-no for me).

Y our life would have meant nothing if you spent it doing things that made you unhappy.

Another important thing I want you to learn is that- yes, there are many evil people in this world, but there are also many good people who always seem to stumble and fall into our lives at the most unexpected moments, and we don't usually realize it then, but their timing is often perfect. I believe one of my favorite fictional characters said it best when he stated that:

"As with all evil, some good will always come from it. It can bring us together with some of the most dedicated, honorable, kind-hearted people we could ever hope to meet. It can fill hearts with love so strong that it will endure forever... and create unbreakable friendships that will last even in the face of life's most difficult challenges. Sometimes, the good comes when we most need it, and least expect it. If we are lucky enough to notice it, set our eyes upon it and appreciate it, it can almost make us forget all of the bad. Today is life. The only life you're sure of. Make the most of today."

-Detective Mac Taylor, *CSI: NY*

(Season 9, Episode 17).

I n the world we live in today it can be very hard at times to believe that there are people who at their cores are genuinely good, but I know that there are out there. Life is tough; I totally get it. All of us are going to have highs and lows, wins and losses, good days and bad days that make us feel like sh*t, but quite frankly- life wasn't meant to be perfect, just like human beings. We were never expected to be these flawless robots. It was never intended to be a smooth ride with no crazy bumps in the road. Our lives would be incredibly boring if it were that way.

Just try to live your best life. Find a group of people who make you happy and who love you unconditionally- the kind of love that says "I will take a bullet for you," or the 3 a.m conversations, the "I will give you my kidney if it would save your life" kind of love. Agape love. True love. Find your people. The right kind of people. The dedicated and kind-hearted type of people who inspire you to do better and be better every single day of your life. Find yourself a group of people who don't need you to have similar DNA to be considered family. Find yourself those kinds of people. Trust me; they are pretty incredible.

Spend time with people who have a positive influence on you and your well-being. Do things that make you happy. Help those in need. Travel. Work hard in whatever field (s) you choose. Speak up for what is right.

And most importantly, never let anyone make you feel

inferior or that your existence doesn't matter. I can assure you we all have our role in this show. We all have our place in the circle of life. You are important, and people do love and care for you (whether you realize that or not)

Create YOUR legacy, one that is worth remembering because at the end of the day we have no control over who lives, and who dies, and who tells our story. Thank you for sticking with me on this adventure. I wish you all the best.

UNTIL WE MEET AGAIN...

18

The Meaning of the Title

THE WHOLE IDEA of the title "*From Dust to Breath*" relates back to the quote from *Genesis*; that you are as dust and when you die, you will return as dust. However, the underlying meaning of my title is that you come from nothing and through life experiences, hard work, and all of the things that shape a human being: become something. A living, breathing being that has the power to make a difference. With your voice. With your actions. With the power within you. And only you can dictate how the breath is used before it is returned to dust. *From Dust to Breath* was created on the whole basis of empowering people to be the best, or at least a better version of themselves. Whenever you feel down remember this, you were once nothing, but now, there is a rare gift within you: the breath of life. Never doubt your worth. You were brought onto this earth for a reason. It may take time to figure out for what purpose, but one day you'll know why.

A Wish

"*May you always have*

Grace in your step,

Song in your hand,

and

Aloha in your heart."

-HAWAIIAN PROVERB

Notes for Reader

Notes for Reader

Notes for Reader

Your Bucket List

This page is for you to list 15 things you have always wanted to do. Once you have completed writing this list, go on to the next page and create a plan on how you will accomplish the activities you wrote down.

Plans

About the Author

Melina Farahmand is a sixteen-year-old American activist, writer, and video editor based in Los Angeles, California. Not only is she a published writer, but Melina is also the founder of *Past Present Future,* a company with the goal of empowering the present and future generations of women.

Aside from being a vocal activist and a dedicated writer and editor, she also has interests in law + social justice, and a passion for filmmaking and directing. Once she completes school, Melina would like to serve as a legal officer in the United States Navy, while continuing her passion for activism and creating + directing stories that will make an impact.

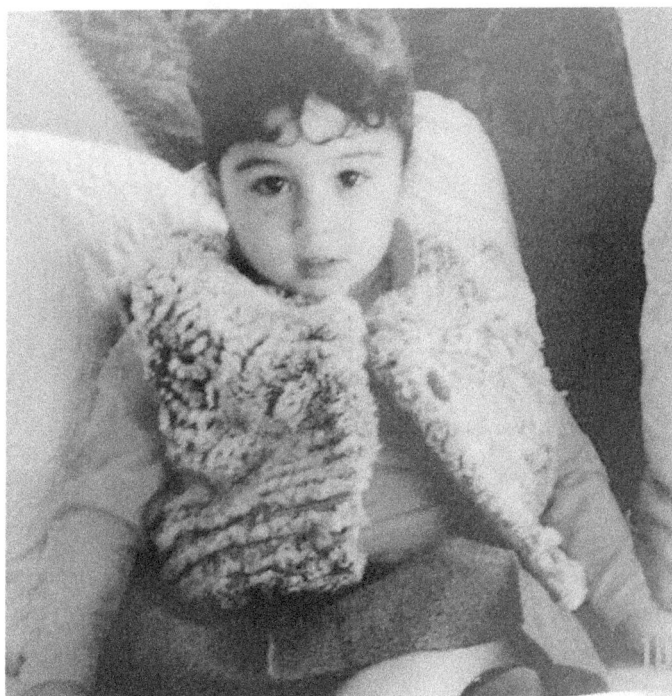

And one day
the girl with the books
became the woman
writing them.